YOUR KNOWLEDGE HAS VALUE

- We will publish your bachelor's and master's thesis, essays and papers

- Your own eBook and book - sold worldwide in all relevant shops

- Earn money with each sale

Upload your text at www.GRIN.com
and publish for free

Bibliographic information published by the German National Library:

The German National Library lists this publication in the National Bibliography; detailed bibliographic data are available on the Internet at http://dnb.dnb.de .

This book is copyright material and must not be copied, reproduced, transferred, distributed, leased, licensed or publicly performed or used in any way except as specifically permitted in writing by the publishers, as allowed under the terms and conditions under which it was purchased or as strictly permitted by applicable copyright law. Any unauthorized distribution or use of this text may be a direct infringement of the author s and publisher s rights and those responsible may be liable in law accordingly.

Imprint:

Copyright © 2014 GRIN Verlag
Print and binding: Books on Demand GmbH, Norderstedt Germany
ISBN: 9783668738645

This book at GRIN:

https://www.grin.com/document/429932

Saskia Schäfers

The Weird Sisters in Macbeth. Supernatural Fates or Common Witches?

GRIN Verlag

GRIN - Your knowledge has value

Since its foundation in 1998, GRIN has specialized in publishing academic texts by students, college teachers and other academics as e-book and printed book. The website www.grin.com is an ideal platform for presenting term papers, final papers, scientific essays, dissertations and specialist books.

Visit us on the internet:

http://www.grin.com/

http://www.facebook.com/grincom

http://www.twitter.com/grin_com

1. Introduction

The play *Macbeth* tells the story of an honourable Scottish soldier who turns into an ambitious murderer in conquest of the Scottish throne over the course of the play. The opening scene of the play introduces three witches also known as the three Weird Sisters. The sisters are believed to be the cause of Macbeth's downfall. By uttering their prophecy at the beginning of the play, stating that Macbeth will first be made a thane and then become king of Scotland, they set in motion the action of the play. The witches role is crucial to the play as they continue to deceive Macbeth and lure him into committing several serious crimes. Ultimately it is debatable if they are the ones responsible for his downfall or if his interpretation of the prophecies and the way that he acted according to them was the deciding element, but this should not be the topic of this paper.

This paper focuses not on the role of the witches in the downfall of Macbeth, but on the nature of the witches themselves. During the Early Modern period when the play was written, the belief in witchcraft was still an actual part of people's lives. The weird sisters in *Macbeth* bear resemblance to the witches persecuted all over Europe during Shakespeare's time. It is important to understand though that they represent much more than just a gruesome copy of those witches. The function and presentation of the Weird Sisters in *Macbeth* is multifaceted and ambiguous.

Therefore the main focus of this paper is to display and contrast the different interpretations of the nature of the three Weird Sisters. There are different opinions as to what the inspiration for Shakespeare was when he created them. One of them is that the three Weird Sisters represent the three Fates that can be found in different mythologies, like the Moraie in Greek mythology or the Norns of Norse mythology. These figures are supposed to have the ultimate knowledge about man's destiny and control over his fate. Another one would be the characterization of the witches as typical and contemporary English, Scottish or Continental witches according to their presentation in the play.

This paper will show the justifications for both of these theories. I maintain the view point that Shakespeare disguised the Weird Sisters as witches in order to make them more familiar to his contemporary audience, an audience for which the belief in witchcraft was real. Their function in the play is therefore that of the Fates, uttering prophecies of his future to Macbeth, but their appearance and behaviour let them look like ordinary witches. Shakespeare's reasons for this masquerade will also be outlined in this paper.

2. The Witches

This paper will first identify the main characteristics for witches during this period and then examine how these apply to the witches portrayed in *Macbeth*.

There was a definite stereotype of witches during this period. Two factors that are very noticeable when describing this stereotype are gender and age. Witches were likely to be female, as the weaker sex would give into satanic temptations more easily, and also old. This is due to the fact that it often took years to build up a reputation as a witch and sometimes senility could have explained the strange behaviour witnessed by neighbors (cf. Levack 129). Witches were likely to have a lowly social and economical status. They were often poor and living on the margins of society. At times they would have to beg to supplement their small income and in order to survive. This poverty made them more amenable for the proposals of the devil (cf. Levack 134).

In *Macbeth*, Banquo describes the appearance of the witches when they first encounter them. First he comments on their age calling them "withered" (1.3.38) which leads to the conclusion that they are of old age. Their clothing is probably in a bad state since he says that they look "wild in their attire" (1.3.38) and generally states that they do not look like they are alive and belong in this world (cf. 1.3.39-41). He attributes to them "choppy fingers" (1.3.42) and "skinny lips" (1.3.43) which would both indicate that they are rather ugly. Lastly, he says that he believes them to be women, but questions their gender by pointing out that they have beards (1.3.44). All these characteristics correspond to the contemporary stereotype of witches.

Witches were often associated with brewing "portions and unguents" that could be harmful to their enemies and neighbours. Levack says that "witches are often portrayed standing over cauldrons, for it was such vessels that many of the agents of sorcery were in fact concocted" (127). This stereotype was used in Macbeth, the stage directions say "A cavern. In the middle a boiling cauldron." (5.1).

As far as their personality is concerned, witches are described as "sharp-tongued, bad-tempered and quarrelsome" (cf. Levack 136). This kind of behaviour can be observed in Shakespeare's witches. In Act 1 Scene 3, when the witches talk about what they have been doing, one of them says that she had met a sailor's wife which refused her some of her chestnuts and told her to go away. This causes the witches to plan revenge on her by causing her husband to encounter a storm, stating "his bark...shall be tempest-tossed" (1.3.23-24). This behavior clearly shows the bad-tempered and quarrelsome character traits that were mentioned above.

Witches and their power are linked to necromancy, the use of body parts of corpses for their spells and portions (cf. Purkiss 126). This also occurs in *Macbeth*. The witches use several body parts among them also "the finger of birth-strangled babe" (1.5.29). This is yet another connection to the contemporary stereotype of witches. Death during birth or at a very young age was a common occurrence in medieval times but for the people at that time often inexplicable. They were looking for someone to blame and this blame was often directed against midwives. They were accused of killing the children, using them for satanic rituals and sacrificing them to the Devil (cf. Levack 127-128).

As one can see there are more than a few parallels between the witches of Shakespearan times and those that Macbeth encounters in the play. They fit into the stereotype according to their outward appearance, their character traits and behaviour as well as by conducting typical rituals while using stereotypical means of sorcery.

3. The Weird Sisters

It has already been stated above that the Weird Sisters, based on their characterization and behaviour in the play, could have been a copy of contemporary witches. There is another theory which favors them to impersonate first and foremost the three Weird Sisters and says that "the Wyrdes, the Norns, the Fates, the Moraie, the Parcae and the Sibyls are all part of Shakespeare's Weird Sisters" (Shamas 98). All these mythological figures have knowledge about the future and utter prophecies about the destiny of man.

The first indicator of this theory is that the Weird Sisters are not actually called witches in the play. The stage directions refer to them as witches and their speech headings are First, Second and Third Witch. In the play itself though they are only called witches once, when the First Witch encounters a sailor's wife and she says "Aroint thee,witch" (1.3.5). When they talk to each other, they address themselves as sisters and Banquo and Macbeth also use the word sisters, not witches, to refer to them (cf. Whalen 60). Whalen concludes this argument by saying that "if priority is given to the spoken words of the play, these characters are primarily the prophesying Weird Sisters with alter egos as Scottish witches" (60).

Another interesting fact is that the word "weird" itself had a different meaning in Shakespeare's time than it does today. Today we would associate it with strange, bizarre or freaky which would favor an interpretation of the Weird Sisters as witches since these are attributes that one would assign to a witch. In Old English the word "weird" or "wyrd" meant "destiny" or "fate" and this was the meaning that Shakespeare would have been familiar with at the time (Whalen 61). Tolman remarks that in "Anglo-Saxon literature "Wyrd" is the name of the personified goddess of fate" (89). Therefore it can be said that the Weird Sisters can be linked to the goddesses of Fate by the meaning of their name.

One of Shakespeare's sources for Macbeth were Holinshed's "Chronicles of England, Ireland and Scotland" which were published in 1577 (cf. Tolman 90). In this publication, the story of Macbeth is described and his encounter with the Weird Sisters as well. Holinshed states the women that they encounter are "the weird sisters, that is (as ye would say) the goddesses of destinie, or else some nymphs or feiries indued with knowledge of phrophesie by their necromatnicall science" (Tolman 91). This description of the Weird Sisters does not align with the presentation of them as witches in Shakespeare's *Macbeth*.

There is also a picture of the Weird Sisters in *Holinshed's Chronicles* "depicting them as the supernatural Fates, not as witches" (Whalen 61). This picture shows them as well dressed and elegant women, not the ugly and bearded witches that occur in Shakespeare's *Macbeth*. In conclusion these arguments indicate that the Weird Sisters were originally Fates, powerful creatures with knowledge of the future and Shakespeare changed their appearance in his play.

Tolman argues that the Weird Sisters can be identified with the Norns of Norse mythology. These women are called Urthr, Verthandi and Skuld whereas these names signify that they represent the Past, Present and Future. Therefore they have extensive knowledge about every man's destiny. He further elaborates that it becomes clear in *Macbeth* that the Weird Sisters impersonate the Norns while they utter their first prophecy to Macbeth. Urthr, the Past, addresses him as the Thane of Glamis which he was before the battle. Verthandi, the Present, addresses him as Thane of Cawdor which is the title that he has now earned with his achievements on the battlefield. He himself does not now of this new title yet. Finally Skuld, the Future, tells him "all hail, Macbeth, thou shalt be king hereafter" (1.3.48). This theory is very plausible, given that the events that the Weird Sisters propecied happened accordingly. Tolman further supported his argument by stating that, even though not as obvious, they also take on the role of the Norns when talking to Banquo about his fate (cf. Tolman 92).

For Whalen it is clear that the Weird Sisters play a double role in the play. They switch from being the supernatural Fates to common, vulgar witches multiple times throughout the play. For him the the reason for this double role, in his opinion, is that the should portray "comical, outrageous witches whose antics undermine the prophecies of the their Weird-Sisters alter egos" (Whalen 66).

As one can see, there is a popular opinion among Shakespeare scholars that the witches in Macbeth are first and foremost the Weird Sisters, supernatural Fates, which are disgraced by being presented as common witches.

4. Reasons for Shakespeare's portrayal of the Weird Sisters as witches

The differences and similarities between the stereotypical witches and Shakespeare's Weird Sisters have already been presented, but it is equally as important to also have a look at the question of what could have influenced him to portray them in this manner. A big influence on the play could have been King James and his patronage to Shakespeare. King James I was crowned king of England in 1603 and quickly became the patron to Shakespeare's acting company the King's Servants which were later known as the King's Men. This patronage was profitable to Shakespeare and his writing and the wish to please the king could have been influential to his works, one of them being *Macbeth*.

To understand the connection between the James I and the play, his personal infliction with witchcraft have to be explained. In 1591, while he was still king of Scotland, he published a pamphlet titled *Newes from Scotland declaring the damnable life and death of Doctor Fian, a notable Sorcerer*. It is based on the North Berwick trials in which three hundred witches were accused of plotting the murder of King James VI. This pamphlet gives a supposed reason for the storm that the king and his wife encountered on their journey to Scotland back from Denmark. Agnis Sampson one of the accused witches confessed to having thrown a cat, christened and with body parts of a dead man bound to it, into the sea. Their intention was to call up a storm and drown King James. (cf. Calhoun 185).

James published another work on witchcraft, titled *Daemonolgie*, which was published in 1597 in Scotland and also in England after his coronation in 1603. His work is divided into three parts: magic and necromancy, witchcraft and sorcery and other spirits and spectres. The book shows his strong beliefs and fear about witchcraft. (cf. Calhoun 185). As a result of this fear of witchcraft, he instituted a law in 1604 which amongst other things prohibited the use of any body part of a corpse in rituals of witchcraft (cf. Tolman 98). The witches accused in the North Berwick trials supposedly used the parts of a dead man's body for their spell which shows the personal connection of James I to this law.

There are several scenes in *Macbeth* that can be linked to King James and witchcraft. A direct reference to the king's book *Daemonolgie* can be found when the witches first meet Macbeth and Banquo and the witches suddenly disappear after they talk to them. Banquo compares them to bubbles that suddenly varnish (cf.1.3.77). In *Daemonolgie* the king explains that witches are "inuisible to anie other, except among themselves" when they are flying (Daemonologie 32). This serves as an example that Shakespeare could have had the Scottish witches, as perceived by king James and his contemporaries, in mind when he created the three Weird Sisters for his play.

There is other evidence for this theory in the cauldron scene where the witches brew together a potion that includes the "liver of a blaspheming Jew" (5.1.26), "Nose of Turk and Tatar's lip"(5.1.29), "poisoned entrails"(5.1.5) and the "finger of a birth-strangled baby"(5.1.30). These are all clearly body parts which are used for witchcraft and according to Calhoun that is "a reflection of James's law against witchcraft" (186). This is an act of necromancy, a topic which was also extensively discussed in *Daemonolgie*. Therefore it is possible that Shakespeare was inspired or influenced by either the law or the the kings publications to include necromancy in the witch scenes.

Another ingredient that they used for their portion also exhibits a connection to King James. The witches namely use a "toad that under cold stone/ Days and nights has thirty-one/ Sweltered venom sleeping got" (5.1.6-8) for their brew. Calhoun again links this to the North Berwick trial and Angie Simpsons confession where she states that she collected toad's venom with the intention of using it to poison the king (186). The connection here is less explicit since the methods of gathering the toad's venom are different, but it is still possible that this is a reference to this incident. King James might have recognized this as allusion to the attempted assassination.

Another allusion that could have been recognized by King James is the close association of the witches with the changes in weather as well as the power they have in changing the weather. There are multiple scenes which refer to this section of witchcraft belief. The one most closely connected to king James would be the third scene of the first act when the witches talk to each other about what they have been doing. One of them wants to get revenge on a sailor's wife which refused to give her chestnuts. She wants to do this by guiding her husband's ship into a storm where it shall be "tempest-tossed"(1.3.24) which means thrown into a storm. As earlier explained King James had accused witches of causing a storm on his journey back from Denmark in 1591 with the intention of killing him, so this scene bears a close resemblance to this incident.

Having investigated the similarities between the witches in the play itself and those King James was confronted with, it can be said that they exhibit a lot of common qualities. Shakespeare could have specifically used and altered material from James' publications in order to please his patron with this play.

Another reason as to why Shakespeare would choose to represent the Weird Sisters, goddesses of fate, as ordinary Elizabethan witches is explained by Tolman in his book *Views about Hamlet and other essays*. He says that "the sense of reality is essential to as serious drama"(100). Shakespeare's dramas are so appealing to his contemporary audiences and audiences today, because their heroes are humanized and provide a "portrayal of real life" (Tolman 101). For Tolman this is one of the reasons why Shakespeare represented the Weird Sisters, to some extent, as common witches. If they were to be perceived as the goddesses of Fate, it would mean that they are the ones that direct and dominate the play. This would interfere with the story, because then Macbeth's actions would be determined by the Weird Sisters and not by himself. Therefore in order to fit into a Shakespearean drama, it was necessary that "they [the Weird Sisters] be made completely real, that they be humanized in some form" (Tolman 101). Shakespeare chose to do this by bestowing characteristics of a witch upon them, the ugliness and stereotypical behaviour.

Hudson also provides an explanation for the changed language and behaviour of the witches in the cauldron scene. He says that the witches know that Macbeth is going to seek them out again and question them and therefore

> they adopt, for the occasion, the sacraments of witchcraft, because they are the only sacraments whereby they can impart to him the Satanic grace and efficacy which it is their office to d dispense. […] This their appalling infernal liturgy is a special and necessary accommodation to the senses and mind of the person they are dealing with. (Hudson 130)

This indicates that the reason for the Weird Sisters, at least in this scene, to behave like common witches, is so that they can communicate with Macbeth in a way that he could understand. He would not be familiar with the religion of the Weird Sisters, but he is indeed familiar with the rituals that they show him in this scene. Tolman supports Hudson's theory by saying that it had to be done in this manner, because when Shakespeare wrote *Macbeth* "the entire people, king and subjects, believed in the reality of witchcraft" (Tolman 102). In conclusion, this means that in order to be properly understood by not only Macbeth in the play, but also the audience, the Weird Sisters had to be transformed into witches. Shakespeare accomplished this by letting them use the "apparatus of witchcraft" (Tolman 92).

5. Conclusion

When looking at the arguments presented above, it can be concluded that the Weird Sisters in Macbeth really bear a strong resemblance to the stereotypical witch of the seventeenth century. This resemblance only applies to the outward appearance and superficial behaviour of the witches though. In my opinion, the Weird Sisters ultimately represent supernatural Fates. Their main function is to utter prophecies, those prophecies that deceive Macbeth into committing several murders and becoming crazy. This function can ultimately and logically be linked to mythological Fates rather than common witches. The occupation of common witches was far inferior, they were not known to influence men to this extent. This is the work of a far higher power.

Shakespeare's sources, especially *Holinshed's Chronicles*, portray the weird sisters in a far more elaborate manner. It is Shakespeare who transforms them into vulgar and common creatures, those known to men during the Elizabethan period. Their name alone tells us that they are far more than that, they are the narrators of fate with ultimate knowledge of man's destiny. This is what they originated from and they still fulfill this function in *Macbeth*. Shakespeare only disguised them.

There are several reasons that I find plausible as to why Shakespeare decided to alter the persona of the Weird Sisters. First of all, the audience of the Elizabethan period firmly believed in witchcraft, it was reality for them. This has to be kept in mind when we look at the Weird Sister. The audience would not have recognized them for what they are, but it did recognize the witches they were disguised as. They were aware of the stereotypical behaviour of witches and so the witches that Macbeth encounters are familiar to them. This is, in my opinion, very important, because Shakespeare wrote his plays to please his contemporary audience.

Another argument that was outlined in this paper is the link between Shakespeare, *Macbeth,* King James and witchcraft. A lot of the witch scenes in *Macbeth* can, as explained in this paper, easily be linked to what the King personally experienced regarding witchcraft. Since he was patron to Shakespeare and his company it would make sense for Shakespeare to use this in his advantage and construct the witches according to James' publications and experiences.

The strongest argument in this matter in my opinion though, is that Shakespeare modified the nature of the Weird Sisters out of dramatic necessity. One of the most important factors in his plays is their strong resemblance to real life. The audience can identify with the tragic protagonist of his plays, like Macbeth. If supernatural powers, like the Weird Sisters who control destiny were to enter that play, it would seem like they were the ones deciding what happens and this would defeat the purpose of the play. The witches, however, do not have that kind of power and can therefore exist in the play. He uses the stereotype of the common and vulgar witch that was not a respectable part of society to discredit the Weird Sisters. This is the only way that they can be part of the play without disturbing the manner of a Shakespearean drama.

In conclusion, this means that the Weird Sisters are in fact the goddesses of destiny. However, they were to an extend transformed by Shakespeare in order to fit into his version of *Macbeth*.

6. Bibliography

Primary Sources

Shakespeare, William. *Macbeth*. Berlin: Cornelsen, 2012. Print.

Secondary Sources

Calhoun, Howell V. "James I and the witch scenes in *Macbeth*". *The Shakespeare Association Bulletin* 17.4 (1942): 184-189. *JSTOR*. Web. 03 March 2015.

Hudson, Henry N. *The complete works of William Shakespeare : with a life of the poet, explanatory foot-notes, critical notes, and a glossarial index*. Boston: Ginn & Heath. 1881. *Internet Archive*. Web. 03 March 2015.

King James the First. *Daemonologie*. ed. by G.B Harrison. New York: Bodley Head Quartos. 1924. Print.

Levack, Brian P. *The Witch-Hunt in Early Modern Europe*. London and New York: Longman, 1987. Print.

Purkiss, Diane. *The Witch in History: Early Modern and Twentieth Century Representations*. London and New York: Routledge, 1996. Print.

Shamas, Laura. *We three: The Mythology of Shakespeare's Weird Sisters*. New York: Lang, 2007.

Showerman, Earl. "Shakespeare's Greater Greek: Macbeth and Aeschylus Oresteia". *Brief Chronicles III* (2011): 37-70. JSTOR. Web. 20 February 2015.

Tolman, Albert H. *The reviews about Hamlet and other essays*. Boston: Houghton Mifflin, 1906. *Internet Archive*. Web. 03 March 2015.

Whalen, Richard. "The Scottish/ Classical Hybrid Witch in Macbeth". *Brief Chronicles IV* (2012-13): 59-72. *JSTOR*. Web. 20 February 2015.

YOUR KNOWLEDGE HAS VALUE

- We will publish your bachelor's and master's thesis, essays and papers

- Your own eBook and book - sold worldwide in all relevant shops

- Earn money with each sale

Upload your text at www.GRIN.com
and publish for free